EXPLORING WORLD CULTURES

Panama

By Sadie Silva

Cavendish Square
New York

Published in 2022 by Cavendish Square Publishing, LLC
29 East 21st Street, New York, NY 10010

First Edition

Website: cavendishsq.com

Library of Congress Cataloging-in-Publication Data

Names: Silva, Sadie, author.
Title: Panama / Sadie Silva.
Description: First Edition. | New York : Cavendish Square Publishing, 2022. | Series: Exploring world cultures | Includes index.
Identifiers: LCCN 2020039631 | ISBN 9781502662316 (Library Binding) | ISBN 9781502662293 (Paperback) | ISBN 9781502662309 (Set) | ISBN 9781502662323 (eBook)
Subjects: LCSH: Panama--Juvenile literature. | Panama--Description and travel. | Panama--History--Juvenile literature. | Panama--Social life and customs.
Classification: LCC F1563.2 .S58 2022 | DDC 972.87--dc23
LC record available at https://lccn.loc.gov/2020039631

Editor: Caitie McAneney
Copyeditor: Jill Keppeler
Designer: Rachel Rising

The photographs in this book are used by permission and through the courtesy of: Cover, Danny Lehman/The Image Bank/Getty Images; p. 4 helovi/E+/Getty Images; p. 5 Javier Fernández Sánchez/Moment/Getty Images; p. 6 Genna Di Franco/EyeEm/Getty Images; p. 7 Eddie Gerald/Moment/Getty Images; p. 8 Historical/Contributor/Corbis Historical/Getty Images; p. 9 Bettmann/Contributor/Getty Images; p. 10 Oswaldo RIVAS/Pool/AFP/Getty Images; p. 11 Comstock Images/Stockbyte/Getty Images; p.12 Zoya Stafienko/Moment/Getty Images; p. 13 Akaradech Pramoonsin/Moment/Getty Images; p. 14 Powerfocusfotografie/Moment/Getty Images; p. 15 Glowimages/Getty Images; p. 16 Blaine Harrington III/ The Image Bank/Getty Images; p. 17 Anton_Ivanov/Shutterstock.com; p. 18 Marc Guitard/Moment/Getty Images; p. 19 Bas Urrutia/EyeEm/Getty Images; p. 20 Enzo Figueres/Moment Open/Getty Images; p. 21 Mondadori Portfolio/Contributor/ Getty Images; p. 22 Jeff Greenberg/Contributor/Universal Images Group/Getty Images; pp. 23, 25 LUIS ACOSTA/ Contributor/AFP/Getty Images; p. 24 Peety Cooper/Stockbyte/Getty Images; p. 26 Paul Henderson Photography/Moment Open/Getty Images; p. 27 Image Source/Getty Images; pp. 28, 29 Sergio Amiti/Moment/Getty Images.

CPSIA compliance information: Batch #CW22CSQ: For further information contact Cavendish Square Publishing LLC, New York, New York, at 1-877-980-4450.

Printed in the United States of America

Contents

Introduction

Panama has been called the crossroads of the world. Located in Central America, this country is on a piece of land that connects North and South America. For much of its history, it was home to indigenous, or native, groups such as the Kuna, Guaymi, and Chocó peoples. Then, Europeans **colonized** the area, and the United States built the Panama Canal. This man-made waterway allows people to easily travel between the Atlantic Ocean and the Pacific Ocean.

Panama City is the most important city in Panama.

Some people live in Panama City, while others live in rural settings, including grasslands and rain forests. Panama is a place of trade and **diverse** cultures. Indigenous, Spanish, African, and North American cultures mix in this country. The result is lively music, arts, and festivals that unite the people of Panama.

Panama is home to diverse plant and animal life.

Geography

Panama is a tropical place. It has warm weather.

Panama is on an isthmus. An isthmus is a thin land bridge that connects two larger areas of land. The Central American country of Costa Rica is to the northwest, while the South American country of Colombia is to the southeast. The Pacific Ocean is to the south and the Caribbean Sea is to the north.

The country is split into provinces, which are like states, and indigenous areas called comarcas.

FACT!

Exotic animals such as red-eyed tree frogs, capybaras, and jaguars live in Panama.

More than 1,500 islands are also part of Panama.

Panama has a diverse landscape. It has beaches and grasslands, or savannas. It also has mountains and **volcanoes**. A wild area called the Darién Gap stretches from Panama into Colombia. It's covered in mountainous rain forests, and only indigenous peoples live there.

Panama's tallest peak, Volcán Barú, rises about 11,400 feet (3,475 meters).

The Wild Darién Gap

There is no road through the wild Darién Gap. It's the one break in the Pan-American Highway, a system of roads through North, Central, and South America.

History

Indigenous peoples have been in Panama for thousands of years. Then, in 1501, Spanish explorers came to the Isthmus of Panama. Soon, Spain settled and colonized the area.

The Panama Canal was built between 1903 and 1914. Thousands of workers died from accidents and illnesses.

The Spanish killed many indigenous people through sicknesses and fighting. Then, they moved south, where they **conquered** the Incas in Peru. They sent Incan gold through Panama to Spain. They brought enslaved

FACT!

The United States controlled the Panama Canal until 1999. Then, Panama took full control.

South American Roots

Panama's culture, or way of life, has South American roots. During the colonial years, it was governed from Peru, and Spain considered it part of Colombia.

Spaniard Vasco Núñez de Balboa became the first European to see the Pacific Ocean in 1513, from today's Panama.

people from Africa to move this gold.

In 1821, Panama became independent from Spain. It was part of Colombia from 1830 to 1903, when it became fully independent. The United States made a deal with Panama to build a canal across the isthmus to link the oceans for trade. Panama became a major world center of trade because of the canal.

Government VOTE ✓

Panama became an independent republic in 1903. A republic is a kind of democracy, or a government in which citizens have a voice. They vote for people called representatives to speak for them.

Mireya Moscoso served as the first female president of Panama from 1999 to 2004.

Everyone in Panama can vote once they reach the age of 18. Panama has a constitution, or a set of laws to keep things fair.

FACT!

Panama City is the capital, or seat of government, of Panama.

Dictatorship

In 1968, Panama's National Guard overthrew the government. This led to a **dictatorship**. Panama became a democracy again in 1990.

Panama's flag has blue and red stars and blue and red squares.

Panama has three branches of government. It has a National Assembly to make laws, a president to carry out laws, and a Supreme Court to judge laws.

Panama has 10 provinces, which are like U.S. states. It also has three comarcas. Comarcas are set aside for indigenous peoples. Provinces are led by governors, and comarcas are led by tribal leaders.

The Economy

A country's economy includes the goods and services that are made, sold, and used. The economy is shaped by **resources** and trade. The Panama Canal shaped the economy of Panama in its early days as an independent nation. It's still shaping it today. Nearly half of the country's income comes from the canal. Ships from around the world use the canal to get from one ocean to the other.

Panama City has tall skyscrapers where many businesses are located.

FACT!

Rural parts of Panama tend to be poorer than cities and the Panama Canal area.

Free Trade

Panama also has the Colón Free Trade Zone. This is the largest free port in the world. This adds service jobs to the country.

Ships have to pay to travel through the canal.

Banking and tourism, or travel, are other important parts of Panama's economy. People work in hotels and restaurants that serve travelers or in the banks where people keep their money. Farming is not as important in Panama as it is elsewhere. However, the main crops include sugar, coffee, corn, and bananas.

Some rural farmers grow coffee to sell.

The Environment

Quetzals are beautiful birds that call Panama home.

Panama is a tropical country. That means the weather is usually very warm. The Caribbean coast of Panama gets a lot of rain. Sometimes powerful storms called hurricanes rip through the area. The savannas to the southwest have less rainfall.

Panama is home to many tropical plants and animals, from sea turtles to rare birds like quetzals

FACT!

People build large mines for copper and gold in Panama. This harms lands and rivers.

Endangered Animals

Some animals in Panama are endangered, or at risk of dying out. The leatherback turtle, ornate spider monkey, and harpy eagle are examples.

and macaws. Because it is on a land bridge, many **species** have moved there throughout history.

Factories and mines in Panama cause pollution.

However, Panama's position as a trade center can harm the environment, or natural world. Water pollution from ships can harm native fish species. Another issue is deforestation, or cutting down trees to build other things. This harms forest animals and plant life. Soil erosion, or the wearing away of soil, is also a big problem.

The People Today

This girl is a member of the Kuna people. They are native to Panama.

Today, most people in Panama live in cities and their surrounding areas. More than half the people in Panama live in and around Panama City and Colón. Only about a third of the people live in rural settings. Some indigenous groups, like the Kuna and Chocó, live in **remote** rain forests and coastal areas.

In 1911, before the Panama Canal opened, the population of Panama was 336,000. Today,

FACT!

The Ngäbe are the largest indigenous group in Panama.

the population is more than 4.3 million! Most people in Panama are a mix of white and indigenous backgrounds, which is sometimes called *mestizo*. Some people of African **descent** also came to Panama. About 12 percent of the population is indigenous.

The Emberá people are native to the Darién Gap.

Many people in Panama are visitors. People from all over the world travel through Panama for trade and tourism!

Building the Population

The Panama City–Colón Railroad and Panama Canal were big building projects. People came from the United States, France, China, and the West Indies to work.

Lifestyle

What is it like to live in Panama? It depends if you live in a busy city or rural area. People in Panama City live in apartment buildings or houses, walk around busy shopping areas, and get around by car, bus, motorcycle, or train. People live 78 years on average. Many people in Panama City are wealthy. However, nearly a quarter of the country of Panama struggles with **poverty**.

This home for a Kuna family sits on one of Panama's tropical islands.

FACT!

The **traditional** Emberá home is called a *bohío*. It has a **thatched** roof.

Women in Panama

Today, women are mostly treated as equal to men in Panamanian culture. The country elected its first female president in 1999.

People who live in rural areas have a very different kind of life. Some indigenous peoples live in smaller villages on islands or in the rain forest. They practice subsistence farming, which means farming only for their families or smaller communities. People's lives are about 10 years shorter in rural areas than in other parts of the country.

Family is very important in Panama.

Religion

People in Panama have the right to practice any religion, or belief system. However, nearly 75 percent of Panamanians practice Roman Catholicism. This was the religion of the Spanish who conquered the region. Some churches still standing today date back to days of the Spanish conquest. The church in Natá de Los Caballeros is said to have been built in the 1500s!

Metropolitan Cathedral in Panama is in Casco Viejo (Old Town), Panama City.

FACT!

Metropolitan Cathedral is one of the largest cathedrals, or grand churches, of Panama.

Leaders of the Church

The Roman Catholic Church has a world leader called the pope, regional leaders called bishops, and leaders of each church called priests.

In the 20th century, there was an increase in the number of Protestant churches. While Christianity is the most popular religion in Panama, other religions also exist there. Panama is home to the largest Jewish community in Central America. Some people practice a mix of Roman Catholic beliefs and West African beliefs called Santería. This religion is practiced in many Caribbean countries.

Pope Francis takes part in World Youth Day in Panama City in 2019.

Language

Signs in Panama are usually in Spanish.

Panama is home to many indigenous languages. When the Spanish arrived in Panama, they spread their language too. Today, Spanish is the official language of Panama. Most people speak Spanish, and some people also speak English. About a third of Panamanians speak an indigenous language, as well as Spanish.

Dialects are variations, or differences, in speech from place to place. There are different Spanish dialects around the world. Panamanian

FACT!

The name Panama comes from an indigenous word said to mean "abundance of fish."

Spreading Language

About 14 percent of Panamanians speak English. The language spread with the building of the Panama Canal and the U.S. presence in Panama.

The Ngäbe people of Panama speak the Ngäbere language.

Spanish is a bit different from the Spanish spoken by Europeans. While the root of the language is the same, it sounds more like Spanish spoken in Caribbean countries. These countries include the Dominican Republic, Puerto Rico, and Cuba. Some people in Panama City even combine Spanish words with English words to form a whole new way of speaking.

Arts and Festivals

Panama has a very strong tradition of arts and music. Styles from Latin America, Africa, and indigenous groups mix together to form something unique, or special. Indigenous peoples make woodcarvings, masks, woven baskets, and other crafts. You can see work from Panamanian painters and photographers in galleries and museums in Panama City.

Polleras are traditional dresses often worn for Panamanian celebrations.

Panamanian music often uses many drums.

FACT!

Lent is a 40-day holy period for Catholics. Carnival is the last big celebration before Lent.

African Influence

Afro-Panamanian art often includes colorful paintings and murals. Sometimes these works **depict** slavery and the later movement of free Black people to Panama.

It blends music from Latin America, Africa, and indigenous groups. Traditional Panamanian folk dances, like *el tamborito*, involve a group dancing in a circle.

People take part in the Carnival parade in Panama City.

People in Panama celebrate, or honor, religious holidays such as Easter. A festival, or celebration, before Lent called Carnival has parades, dances, fireworks, and street parties in many areas. A Carnival queen rides on a float in a big parade. Women and girls take part in parades while wearing pollera dresses.

Fun and Play

There are plenty of ways to have fun in Panama! Nature-lovers can check out national parks, such as Darien National Park and Soberania National Park. People can go birding, or search for exotic birds. Beaches and coastal areas are perfect for swimming, surfing, and snorkeling. You can discover exotic sea creatures or visit an island. People who fish for sport can find huge fish off the

People visit Panama's Caribbean coast for snorkeling, scuba diving, and swimming.

FACT!

People who fish can go to Piñas Bay to catch big fish such as marlins, swordfish, and tuna.

Scuba in Panama!

Scuba divers can dive into colorful coral reefs off the Caribbean coast of Panama. They can dive with sharks, whales, and dolphins off the Pacific coast of Panama.

Soccer, called football in Panama, is a popular sport.

coast of Panama. People take part in traditional dancing, music, and festivals, both in Panama City and in smaller towns.

People in Panama play basketball, baseball, and tennis. Many people enjoy baseball in particular. Several Panamanians have played on U.S. baseball teams. As in many Latin American countries, another very popular sport is football, or soccer.

Food

This *sancocho* is flavored with cilantro.

Panamanian dishes often use fish, vegetables, and tropical fruit. Panamanians eat fish dishes like ceviche, which uses raw fish, vegetables, and spicy peppers. They eat fried plantains, which are a tropical fruit much like bananas.

Like other Central American countries, Panama has many dishes made with rice, beans, and corn. People use chiles to make dishes spicy. Many Panamanian dishes also use the herb

FACT!

Panamanian menus often include a fish called corvina.

A Delicious Dish

One famous Panamanian dish is sancocho. This stew has meat (usually chicken) and vegetables. Sancocho is also popular in Colombia and the Dominican Republic.

cilantro for added flavor. Panamanian favorites like tamales and arroz con pollo (rice with chicken) are found throughout Central America. Colombian dishes are also popular in Panama, including *carimañolas* (meat fritters). Caribbean dishes like *yuca al moho* (boiled cassava) are also popular. As with many parts of Panamanian culture, the food is a mixture of all the cultures that have passed through the country!

Panamanians drink a milky, cinnamon-flavored corn drink called *chicheme*.

Glossary

colonize To establish a colony.

conquer To take over.

depict To show something in picture form.

descent The background of a person in terms of their family or nationality.

dictatorship A government run by one person or a small group with absolute power.

diverse Different or varied.

exotic Out of the ordinary.

poverty The state of being poor.

remote Far away.

resource Something that can be used.

species A group of plants or animals that are all the same kind.

thatched Having a roof made of dried plant material.

traditional Following what's been done for a long time.

volcano An opening in Earth's surface through which hot, liquid rock sometimes flows.

Find Out More

Books

Black, Vanessa. *Panama Canal*. Minneapolis, MN: Jump! Inc., 2019.

Perritano, John. *Panama*. New York, NY: Weigl Publishers, 2019.

Website

Panama

kids.nationalgeographic.com/explore/countries/panama/

Explore more facts about Panama with *National Geographic*.

Video

Panama Geography

www.youtube.com/watch?v=9tHyNKbN0Qo

Learn the names of Panama's provinces and regions in this Kids Learning video.

Index

About the Author

Sadie Silva is the author of many books for young people. She enjoys writing, traveling, and reading on the beach.